CULTURE IN ACTION

Journals and Blogging

Jim Mack

Raintree

Chicago, Illinois

www.heinemannraintree.com
Visit our website to find out
more information about
Heinemann-Raintree books.

To order:
☎ Phone 888-454-2279
💻 Visit www.heinemannraintree.com
to browse our catalog and order online.

©2010 Raintree
an imprint of Capstone Global Library, LLC
Chicago, Illinois

Edited by Louise Galpine, Abby Colich, and Laura J. Hensley
Designed by Kimberly Miracle and Betsy Wernert
Original illustrations © Capstone Global Library Ltd.
Illustrated by kja-artists.com
Picture research by Mica Brancic and Kay Altwegg
Production by Alison Parsons
Originated by Dot Gradations Ltd.
Printed in China by Leo Paper Products Ltd

13 12 11 10 09
10 9 8 7 6 5 4 3 2 1

Library of Congress Cataloging-in-Publication Data
Mack, James (James Matthew), 1978-
  Journals and blogging / Jim Mack.
    p. cm. -- (Culture in action)
  Includes bibliographical references and index.
  ISBN 978-1-4109-3406-2 -- ISBN 978-1-4109-3423-9 (pbk)
1. Diaries--Authorship--Juvenile literature. 2. Blogs--Juvenile
literature. I. Title.
  PN4390.M32 2009
  808'.06692--dc22
                          2009000490

Acknowledgments

The author and publishers are grateful to the following for
permission to reproduce copyright material: ©Alamy pp. **4**
(Thinkstock/JupiterImages), **6** (fotovisage), **9** (Adam von
Mack), **10** (Buzzshotz), **11** (Radius Images), **12** (Blend Images),
13 (Inspirestock, Inc.), **15** (Radius Images), **16** (David R.
Frazier Photolibrary, Inc.), **19** (Thinkstock/JupiterImages), **20**
(Howard Barlow), **24** (Enigma), **25** (Paul Doyle), **26** (Pixland/
Jupiter Images), **28** (Lebrecht Music and Arts Photo Library);
©Getty Images pp. **8** (Tanya Constantine), **27** (Jenny Acheson);
©iStockphoto pp. **5**, **7**, **17**; ©PA Photos p. **22** (PA Wire);
©Shutterstock p. **21**; ©www.dailykos.com p. **29**.

Icon and banner images supplied by Shutterstock: © Alexander
Lukin, © ornitopter, © Colorlife, and © David S. Rose.

Cover photograph of a teenage boy leaning against a tree trunk
and working on a laptop reproduced with permission of Getty
Images/DK Stock/David Deas.

We would like to thank Nancy Harris, Jackie Murphy, and
Tristan Boyer Binns for their invaluable help in the preparation
of this book.

Every effort has been made to contact copyright holders of
any material reproduced in this book. Any omissions will be
rectified in subsequent printings if notice is given to
the publisher.

All the Internet addresses (URLs) given in this book were valid
at the time of going to press. However, due to the dynamic
nature of the Internet, some addresses may have changed, or
sites may have changed or ceased to exist since publication.
While the author and publisher regret any inconvenience this
may cause readers, no responsibility for any such changes can
be accepted by either the author or the publisher.

Contents

Some words are printed in bold, **like this**. You can find out what they mean by looking in the glossary on page 30.

Writing from Within

What things are going on in your life right now? Maybe you just found out you are moving to a new house. Or perhaps you are getting a new pet. Did you just read a book you really like or dislike? What did you think about the last movie you saw?

Whether you are writing about important events, your everyday life, or your opinions about the world around you, journals and blogs are a great way to keep a written record of your thoughts, ideas, and opinions. Keeping a journal or blog can be fun. It can help you to better understand yourself and the world around you. It is also a great way to practice writing.

Writing regularly in a journal can help you develop your thoughts. You will be able to think about your feelings more clearly.

Blogging is another way people write down their thoughts and feelings.

Journals versus blogs

Journal writing focuses on you. It is usually kept private. People keep journals to record their thoughts, feelings, and experiences. Writing in a journal regularly can help you see how you have grown as a person.

A blog is like a journal in some ways. It is another place where people write down their thoughts. One major difference between a journal and a blog is that people **upload** (transfer) blogs to a website on the Internet. People write blogs for others to read.

Writing to relieve stress

Writing about personal experiences and feelings is healthy for your mind and body. Journal writing can help relieve stress and help people to sleep better. Good sleeping habits result in more energy and a better memory.

Blogs allow regular people to become a part of the **media**. The media includes major forms of communication such as radio and television. A good blog gives readers entertaining thoughts about news, popular entertainment, and other topics.

Recording Your Life

A journal is an ongoing collection of writings. It can be about personal events, experiences, and feelings. It is a place for you to **reflect**, or think about issues in detail.

Keeping a journal can help you to understand yourself, others, and the world around you. Writing down your thoughts and questions in a journal helps you to think about the things happening in your life. Recording these things will help you to think more about them now. It will also help you to think about them later, when you look back at what you wrote. A journal is for personal use. It is not meant to be read by others, unless you want to share it.

Journal or diary?

Journals and *diaries* are different words for the same thing. Both are places where you can keep a written record of your thoughts and activities.

Just like taking a long walk, writing in a journal can help you clear your head.

Choosing what to write

A journal is a record of your life. But it is not necessarily used to write down everything you do. For example, writing about what you do every morning, like brushing your teeth, is not something that is written about in a journal. Losing your last baby tooth and writing about how it made you feel would be a more appropriate and interesting journal **entry**.

Write it down!

If you have a great idea, thought, or just something you want to remember, write it down in your journal. Otherwise, you may not remember it later.

Journal writing is a way to take a closer look at yourself.

Choose a journal that is lightweight. You might want to carry it with you.

Choosing a journal

A journal is a paper notebook that is flexible, long lasting, and easy to take with you. If a normal-sized notebook is too big to carry with you, use a small notebook to write quick notes. Later, you can record **in-depth** (complete) thoughts in a larger notebook.

Some people use a computer to type their journals. Save the file in a safe, hidden area if you want to keep it private.

What to write?

A journal is about you and your reflections. What you reflect on is up to you. Topics that concern you could include:

- emotions
- your surroundings
- travel
- relationships
- family
- friends
- beliefs.

You can bring your journal everywhere you go, or you can keep it in a safe place at home.

Organizing a journal

One reason to keep a journal is so you can read it again later. It is therefore important to organize your journal in a way that is easy to read and understand. Label each journal entry with a date, time, and location. You might want to separate it into different sections or themes, such as "life at home," "social events," and "friends." You can also write about the setting where you write a journal entry. For example, you can write if it is warm or cold, or if you are on the street or in a building.

No rules

There are many different ways to keep a journal, but there are no rules. You can write every day at a specific time. You can also write whenever you feel like it. If you want, you can also use pictures instead of words (see page 13).

The Journal Journey

Writing in a journal can do more than keep a record of your thoughts and feelings. You can use your journal to help you see how you grow as a person.

Why keep a journal?

You can write about any challenge in your life. Writing can help you understand what you are feeling. For example, maybe an argument with a friend left you feeling frustrated, but you don't know why. If you try to write about what happened, it might help you to sort out your feelings. Focus on writing about exactly what happened. Explore how you reacted each step of the way. For example, maybe your friend made you feel frustrated because he wouldn't listen to your side of the story. This could be what is making you feel so upset afterward.

Everyone experiences conflict. Writing about your conflicts can help you deal with your feelings.

When writing, you will not always figure out why you feel the way you do about a situation. You may have to set your journal aside for days before returning to it for a fresh look. You may write about the same thing over and over again.

Listen to yourself

To learn more about yourself, you will have to **reflect**. Think of an experience you had recently. Now that you can look back on it, how could you have handled the situation differently? In the example of an argument with your friend, maybe you could have calmly asked your friend to stop for a moment and listen to you. These sorts of answers will give you **insight** (more understanding) into how to handle similar situations in the future.

Write comfortably

Whenever you write, you should be calm and relaxed. Before writing, close your eyes and take some deep breaths. Focus on what you want to write about.

Try to write in a comfortable place where there are no distractions.

Dream catching

Some people think dreams are your "inner self" trying to communicate with you. Try exploring your dreams in your journal. It is another way of learning about yourself.

When you wake up, replay your dream in your head. Then write it down. Look for **symbolism** in the dream that relates to your life. For example, if you were alone and scared in the dream, is there a situation in your life that makes you feel the same way? If you had a happy or fun dream, did this reflect positive things going on in your life?

Interpreting dreams

Sometimes dreams are easy to **interpret** (explain)—for example, if a person has a scary dream after watching a scary movie. Other dreams are more difficult to understand.

Even while you sleep, your mind is active. It makes you dream.

Not just words

Writing isn't the only way to learn about yourself. By including drawings and photographs in your journal, you will add more details about what you like and what interests you. Adding items such as newspaper articles, magazine clippings, postcards, and stickers will help you to remember where you were and why you felt how you did. These extra details can allow you to revisit your past more clearly.

More than just paper

Create a recorded journal using a tape recorder or video camera. Record your thoughts and feelings and then listen to or watch the recordings later.

Recording yourself is a fun and easy way to capture your mood and surroundings.

Create a music journal

Music can help to bring out emotions. Music can be very calming. It can also make you feel excited or sad. Writing about how music makes you feel can help you practice journal writing.

Steps to follow:

1. Get your journal or some paper and a pen or pencil.

2. Pick out some music that you like. Find one or more of your favorite songs or your favorite CD. You could also try out new music you have never heard before. Ask an adult if you need help finding something.

3. Find a comfortable place to listen and write. Write the date and time at the top of your journal **entry**.

4. Turn on the music.

5. Relax and close your eyes.

6. Listen closely to the music.

7. Write about the different ways the music makes you feel. Think about what the music reminds you of. A person? An event? Is the music fast or slow? Let your words flow onto the page as you listen. Write freely!

Blogs

Blogs have had a lot of influence on the world. They first appeared on the Internet in the 1990s. Anyone can write a blog about any kind of topic.

What is a blog?

A blog is similar to a journal. But instead of writing in a notebook, it is typed on a computer. Then it is **uploaded** to a website on the Internet. Blogs allow a person to share information and opinions with people from all over the world.

Personal blogs

The type of blog that is most like a journal is the personal blog. Most personal blogs are written frequently. They are written weekly, daily, or even hourly. A personal blog expresses a person's opinions and comments.

A personal blog is written for an audience. Most personal blogs allow public **interaction** (participation) by allowing readers to leave comments. Readers can type and **post** a response that appears on the blog website.

You might have friends or family members who write blogs.

Blogs, blogging, and bloggers

Blog is short for *weblog*. (*Web* is short for *website* or *web page*. A log is a record of something.) The word *blog* can refer to the weblog a person keeps. It can also be used as a verb to mean the act of writing a weblog—for example, you can say that someone blogs for a living. People who blog are called bloggers.

Blogs became popular in part because they can be written anywhere. All you need is a computer and access to the Internet.

The beginning of blogs

In 1994 the earliest blogs were journals and diaries kept online. By 1999 blogging computer **software** was created. These computer programs allowed people to start a blog easily. The Internet was soon flooded with bloggers' voices.

Blogs allow writers to express an opinion about a topic to an audience. Bloggers write about any topic that they feel is important.

All kinds of blogs

Successful blogs usually focus on one **genre**, or category (see box below). Doing so makes it easier to attract an audience that has similar interests and views.

Blogs can be used for almost any form of communication. Photoblogs and sketchblogs are blogs that focus on pictures. These may also have written descriptions. Video blogs, called vlogs, and audio blogs let people see and hear a blogger's **insight** instead of just reading. Mobile blogs, called moblogs, exist for short messages on cell phones and other electronic devices.

Blogs can be written about anything, including fashion. People can express their opinions about different fashion designs in a blog.

Blog topics

Blogs are written about almost anything. There are blogs about personal experiences and blogs that answer questions. There are blogs that discuss fashion, travel, cooking, education, **politics** (issues about government), and the military. Authors, movie stars, athletes, and many other people often have their own blogs.

Sharing your art

Not all blogs are written. Some artists upload copies of their artwork onto blogs for others to see. Other artists use blogging as a form of expression.

You can create art as a way to express your feelings, instead of writing words. Display this work for others to see, just as artists use their blogs.

Artists can use blogs to show other people their art. The Internet creates a huge audience.

Steps to follow:

1. Get a piece of paper and crayons, markers, or whatever else you want to use to create your artwork. You could even make a collage by cutting out pictures from a magazine and gluing them onto the paper.

2. Think about what your artwork will focus on. Do you want to create a picture of an event or person from your life? Or do you want to create a picture of colors, shapes, and lines? If you are in a happy mood, you may feel like creating a bright, colorful picture. If you are in a sad mood, you may want to use darker colors.

3. Create your artwork, then find a place to display it where others can see it. This will allow you to share your ideas and emotions with other people. If you want, write a few lines describing your work and why you created what you did.

The Blog Effect

People who participate in any type of blogging are considered part of a community called the **blogosphere**. The blogosphere is made up of all blogs and bloggers. The blogosphere makes it easy for its members to exchange information by creating **hyperlinks**. These are links to other websites. People can also leave comments for one another on a blog.

What makes a blog popular?

A personal blog can become popular if it is well written, interesting, and updated regularly (usually at least once a week). It also needs **promotion**. Promoting something draws attention to it. A blogger who wants to get noticed will spend time reading and **posting** comments on other blogs. The comments will usually include the website of his or her own blog.

Bloggers are part of a community. Blogs give people an opportunity to discover the thoughts and interests of other people.

Free wireless internet access in this area

REAR
WINDOW

Interesting blogs will gain loyal readers. People will be eager to check a blog for updates—for example, to read news about a travel lover's most recent trip.

VACAY BLOG

a blog for people who love to travel

HOME   FEATURED   TAGS   FIND   CONTACT   ABOUT

Monkey family from the zoo

SUNDAY, JUNE 28

Today our family took a trip to the zoo. Since the zoo is so big, it took our family all day to see everything. We enjoyed all of the animals, but the penguins were definitely our favorite part. Here is a picture of a family of monkeys, which we also really liked. The only bad part is that it was really crowded today. Our family would recommend visiting the zoo on a day when you have time to see everything. There is so much to see!

The Golden Gate Bridge, San Francisco, CA

SUNDAY, JUNE 21

Today we returned home from a family vacation to San Francisco, California. There is a lot for everyone to do in this big, fun city. We rode in a trolley car, drove across the Golden Gate Bridge, went to an aquarium, and saw Alcatraz Island. Alcatraz Island was once a prison. Here is a picture of the Golden Gate Bridge taken during our trip. If you ever get a chance, our family agrees that you should definitely visit this fascinating city.

Bloggers will often have a "blogroll." A blogroll is a list posted on the blogger's page of other blogs he or she supports.

Money for thoughts

Blog writing can become a full-time job for some people. Blogs that stand out may be read by many people. Companies will pay to put product advertisements on popular blogs. Just as people enjoy certain book authors or newspaper reporters, they will keep coming back for more if they like the writing of a particular blogger. A popular blog can help a writer find a good writing job.

Finding a blog

There are more than 100 million active blogs on the Internet. Blog **search engine** websites help users search for interesting blogs. They also give helpful information about everything related to blogs. Blogs usually contain links to other, related blogs. In addition, there are online communities that connect bloggers to one another.

Some bloggers write to bring about change.

Activism

Some bloggers write to try to bring about change. Blogs are a way to promote **activism**, or giving a voice to important issues. For example, environmental activists will bring attention to problems such as unclean water. Activists can use blogs to bring attention to problems in the world such as poverty.

Political impact

People can use **political** blogs to promote politicians and issues. By 2004 political blogging became very popular. Bloggers started getting passes to **media** events that normally were reserved only for reporters. Some blogs question government leaders and policies. Some politicians write blogs to inform others about their views and positions.

Freedom of speech

Some countries have less freedom of speech than others. In 2007 a blogger was jailed in Egypt for writing negatively about his country and the Egyptian president in a blog. In 2008 bloggers in Italy were warned that it is illegal to have an unregistered blog. A 2001 Italian law states that all online publications must first be **registered** (on record) with the government.

PERFORMANCE ACTIVITY

Write a persuasive speech

Many bloggers hope to reach people to bring about change. What is something you would like to change? Write a speech to persuade others to join your cause.

Steps to follow:

1. Get your writing tools ready. Use a pen and paper or a computer. It does not matter what tools you use.

2. Find a comfortable place to write.

3. Start thinking about ideas for a topic to write about. What is an issue that you think needs change? Is it something at school, at home, or in the world?

4. Begin writing your speech. Be sure to explain what the topic is. Then make your case for what needs to be changed and why. Use words that show how much you believe in your cause—for example, "I strongly believe."

5. Read your speech aloud and make sure everything makes sense. Make any desired changes.

6. Share your speech with your class, family, or friends. When reading, speak clearly. Read with feeling and passion.

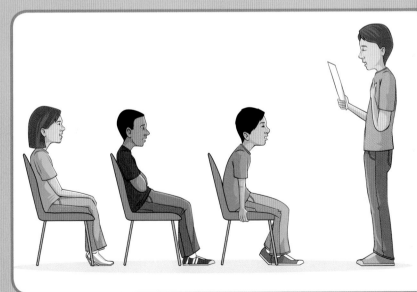

Issues and the Internet

The Internet is a fascinating and useful tool for communication, research, and information. But there are several important issues you need to keep in mind in order to use blogs wisely.

Blogs versus the news

Many people get the news daily through major newspapers or television networks. Most of this news is presented in a fair manner. The reporters state facts about a story without giving their opinions. This allows viewers or readers of the news to come to their own conclusions about a story.

Unlike local television newscasts, blogs are not a reliable source for the news.

Blogs should not be your only source of information. Make sure you read magazines and newspapers as well before you make your mind up about an issue.

Blogs, on the other hand, are normally **biased**. They often only represent the blogger's opinions on the topic he or she is writing about. They may include information that is not factual.

You must keep this in mind when reading blogs. Remember that you are reading opinions, not the news. You need to stay well informed through other, unbiased sources. This will make you truly informed on all sides of an issue.

Digging deeper

At the same time, blogs can help you learn about stories you may not hear about in your local paper or on the evening news. Many bloggers like to find topics that are not being discussed in popular **media**, such as television news. Sometimes new topics become very popular in the **blogosphere**. In this way, bloggers have the power to bring attention to topics that would otherwise be ignored. Blogs can inspire you to look into new issues. You can learn more about them for yourself.

Internet safety

It is also very important to stay safe when reading blogs and using the Internet. Always be aware that dangerous people and messages could appear online, just as in real life. You should never use the Internet without the supervision of a parent or caregiver.

Online safety tips

- Avoid strangers: Visit safe websites and only communicate with people you know.

- Keep it private: Do not share your name, age, school, phone number, address, picture, or passwords with anyone.

- Follow rules: Obey the rules you and your parents discuss. Do not use the Internet to cheat or hurt others.

Always be sure an adult knows what you are doing on the Internet.

- **Download** safely: Always ask a parent or caregiver before you download anything. Some programs online are illegal or can harm your computer.

- Tell someone: Always talk to your parents or caregivers about your experiences on the Internet. Ask them questions and tell them if you are ever scared or uncomfortable.

Spreading the word

Journals and blogs can be started by anyone. There are no rules, requirements, or special knowledge needed. A journal will only cost the price of a notebook. Most blogs are free to start. All people need is a desire to express themselves.

A journal lets you learn about yourself through writing about interests, thoughts, and observations. Journals do not have to be well written. The important thing is finding the wisdom within yourself.

Everyone has their own "voice," or style. Writing can help you find your voice.

Good blogs, on the other hand, are well written and communicate effectively with others. They present ideas about which the blogger has thought long and hard.

Both journals and blogs are tools you can use to help you learn and communicate. Writing is a skill that needs to be practiced. Keeping a journal or blog is an excellent way to gain this practice—and to learn about yourself in the process.

Famous Journal Writers and Bloggers

Journal writers

Throughout history, many people have gained fame for their journal writing.

Mary Shelley (1797–1851)

Mary Shelley was a famous British novelist. She is best known for her book *Frankenstein* (1818). She kept many journals about her life and travels. She wrote a famous travel journal with her husband, the poet Percy Bysshe Shelley, in 1817.

Henry David Thoreau (1817–1862)

Henry David Thoreau was a U.S. author. He kept numerous journals about his thoughts and observations concerning nature and writing. His book *Walden* (1854) details the two years of his life he spent living simply in a small house, observing nature.

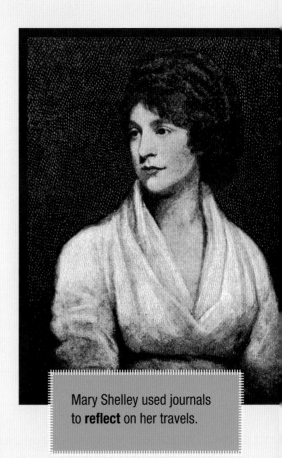

Mary Shelley used journals to **reflect** on her travels.

Anne Frank (1929–1945)

Anne Frank was a young Jewish girl living in Amsterdam, in the Netherlands. She kept a journal between 1942 and 1944 of her experience hiding in an attic with her family. They were hiding from the German army. She wrote about her thoughts, feelings, family, and dreams. After her death, Frank's diary was made into a book and play.

Bloggers

Many people have made successful careers for themselves as bloggers.

Mark Frauenfelder (born 1960)

Mark Frauenfelder is a U.S. journalist, artist, and blogger who cofounded the blog "bOING bOING" in 2000. It focuses on news, technology, art, and politics. In 2003 he moved his family from Los Angeles to the South Pacific, where he blogged about his adventures with his wife and two daughters.

Markos Moulitsas (born 1971)

U.S. writer Markos Moulitsas started a popular **political** blog called "Daily Kos" in 2002. Presidents Jimmy Carter and Barack Obama have contributed their writings to the blog.

Markos Moulitsas's blog has a large community of readers and writers.

Justin Hall (born 1974)

U.S. writer Justin Hall is considered one of the first bloggers. He started blogging in 1994, when blogs were still called online journals or online diaries. For 11 years he blogged about everything in his life, from school to relationships to feelings. Thousands of people read his blog every day.

Glossary

activism taking action to achieve a goal, often for a social or political cause. People interested in environmental activism can use blogs to spread their ideas.

biased supporting only one opinion. Blogs are often biased.

blogosphere interconnected community of all blogs. The blogosphere brings people together from all over the world.

download transfer information from a large computer to a smaller device. People download software from the Internet to their home computers.

entry written record or account of something. A journal entry can be short or long.

genre class or category. Successful blogs usually focus on one genre, such as travel.

hyperlink link on a website that leads to a file or other page. Hyperlinks to other blogs are a common feature of blogs.

in-depth complete. An in-depth journal entry would deeply explore a subject.

insight more understanding. Writing in a journal can give you insight into why you feel a certain way.

interaction participation through communication. Interaction occurs among millions of people every day on the Internet.

interpret explain or give meaning to. An interpretation of a dream may help to shed light on what is happening in your everyday life.

media any form of mass communication, such as radio, television, newspapers, and magazines. The Internet has changed the way the media works.

political having to do with a government. Political blogs help people to learn about issues and candidates.

politics relating to governments and the groups that work to achieve goals through governments. Many blogs are written about politics.

post enter or publish text, data, or other information on the Internet. Some people react to blogs by posting comments about them.

promotion way of drawing attention to something by advertising it or making it public. It is important to promote a blog to let people know about it.

reflect think about a subject in detail. Writing in a journal is one way to reflect on what happens in your life.

register record something with someone, such as a government. Some countries require blogs to be registered with the government.

search engine website that searches the Internet for a specific topic. People find blogs about topics they are interested in by using search engines.

software computer program. Word-processing software will help you with your writing on a computer.

symbolism using symbols to show deeper, special, or hidden meaning. Sometimes dreams hold symbolism for something else happening in a person's life.

upload transfer data to the Internet using a computer. Some artists upload their artwork as a kind of blog.

Find Out More

Books

Garfield, Patricia L. *Dream Catcher: A Young Person's Journal for Exploring Dreams.* Plattsburgh, N.Y.: Tundra, 2003.

Oxlade, Chris. *My First Internet Guide* (*My First Computer Guides*). Chicago: Heinemann Library, 2008.

Wan, Guofang. *Virtually True: Questioning Online Media* (*Media Literacy*). Mankato, Minn.: Capstone, 2007.

Websites

Anne Frank House
www.annefrank.org

Blogging: The Phenomenon
http://library.thinkquest.org/05aug/01130/

Internet Safety
www.wiredsafety.org/youth.html

Index